TABLE OF CONTENTS

INTRODUCTION

The Rise of AI

In the not-so-distant past, the concept of artificial intelligence (AI) was confined to the realms of science fiction, sparking imaginations with visions of sentient machines and futuristic landscapes. Today, we stand at the precipice of an unprecedented era—the rise of AI, a technological revolution reshaping the very fabric of our existence. As algorithms evolve and machines exhibit increasingly sophisticated cognitive abilities, we find ourselves confronted by a profound question: will AI surpass human intelligence?

"The Turing Dilemma: Navigating the Future of Artificial and Human Intelligence" embarks on a journey to explore the intricate interplay between man and machine. From the historical roots of AI to the ethical quandaries posed by its rapid ascent, this book delves into the heart of the Turing Dilemma—a nuanced inquiry into the coexistence, collaboration, and potential clashes between human and artificial intelligence. As we navigate this uncharted territory, we seek not only to understand the technological landscape that surrounds us but also to discern our role in shaping a future where intelligence knows no bounds

THE BIG QUESTION!

WILL AI REPLACE HUMANS' INTELLIGENCE?

The Turing Dilemma: Navigating the Future of Artificial and Human Intelligence

JAMES BRANDY

CHAPTER ONE

Unraveling the Threads of Intelligence

In the tapestry of existence, intelligence stands as a defining thread, woven intricately into the essence of humanity. As we embark on this journey of understanding, we are compelled to unravel the enigma that is intelligence, exploring its manifestations in both human and artificial realms.

The chapter opens with an exploration of the multifaceted nature of human intelligence—its cognitive intricacies, emotional nuances, and adaptive capacities. From the complexities of problem-solving to the subtleties of emotional intelligence, we peel back the layers that make human minds extraordinary.

Simultaneously, we venture into the realm of artificial intelligence, where algorithms and machine learning algorithms strive to replicate and augment cognitive functions. The dichotomy between the organic and the engineered becomes apparent, raising questions about the essence of true intelligence and the boundaries of its replication.

Through a historical lens, we trace the evolution of intelligence from ancient philosophies to contemporary neuroscience, laying the foundation for a comparative analysis between human cognition and artificial computational prowess. The chapter culminates in the recognition that our quest for understanding intelligence is not merely an academic pursuit but a journey that holds profound implications for the future coexistence of humans and machines.

CHAPTER TWO

The Turing Test: Bridging Realms of Consciousness

As we navigate the intricate landscape of intelligence, the Turing Test emerges as a bridge connecting the human and artificial domains. Conceived by Alan Turing in 1950, this benchmark challenges our ability to distinguish between human and machine intelligence. In this chapter, we delve into the foundations and implications of the Turing Test, exploring its nuances and impact on our understanding of intelligence.

We begin by revisiting Turing's visionary proposal and the philosophical questions it raises. What does it mean for a machine to exhibit intelligent behavior indistinguishable from that of a human? Can a machine truly comprehend, reason, and communicate with the depth and subtlety inherent in human interaction?

The chapter then ventures into the historical attempts to pass the Turing Test, highlighting both successes and limitations. From early chatbots to contemporary language models, we scrutinize the evolution of artificial intelligence's capacity to simulate human conversation and cognition.

Drawing on insights from cognitive science and linguistics, we dissect the elements that make human communication uniquely intricate. The chapter challenges readers to reflect on the essence of consciousness and self-awareness, pushing the boundaries of what it means to be intelligent.

Ultimately, the Turing Test serves as a pivotal crossroads in our exploration, prompting us to question not only the capabilities of machines but also the essence of human intelligence. As we stand on the precipice of a future where machines strive to emulate the intricacies of our minds, the Turing Test becomes a lens through which we examine the convergence and divergence of two realms of consciousness.

CHAPTER THREE

Beyond the Binary: The Turing Test Unveiled

As we journey deeper into the heart of machine intelligence, Chapter 3 unfolds the layers of the Turing Test, revealing its complexities and the evolving landscape of assessing artificial cognition. The Turing Test, while a landmark concept, beckons us to go beyond a binary perspective, inviting a nuanced exploration of machine capabilities.

The chapter commences with a historical retrospective, tracing the Turing Test's impact on the field of artificial intelligence. We explore its influence on early AI development, from initial attempts to contemporary advancements in natural language processing and machine learning. The narrative unfolds, showcasing the iterative nature of the test and its adaptability to ever-evolving technological landscapes.

A critical examination of the strengths and limitations of the Turing Test follows, challenging preconceived notions about what it truly means to pass or fail. We delve into scenarios where machines may excel in certain aspects of intelligence, yet fall short in others—highlighting the intricacies of assessing machine cognition in a holistic manner.

With the advent of deep learning and neural networks, the chapter navigates through the nuances of how modern AI systems approach the challenges posed by the Turing Test. From chatbots to sophisticated language models, we witness the spectrum of AI capabilities and the ongoing pursuit of creating machines that not only mimic human intelligence but also comprehend its intricacies.

As we explore the rich tapestry of the Turing Test, the chapter sets the stage for a deeper dive into the ethical considerations and societal impacts that arise when machines approach, and sometimes surpass, human-like intelligence. The Turing

Test becomes a portal into a realm where artificial minds beckon us to reevaluate the very essence of cognition.

CHAPTER FOUR

Pioneering the Future: AI's Historical Milestones

In the annals of technological evolution, Chapter 4 unfolds the rich tapestry of historical milestones that have shaped the trajectory of artificial intelligence. From early conceptualizations to groundbreaking achievements, this chapter explores the transformative moments that paved the way for the AI landscape we navigate today.

We commence our journey with the birth of the term "artificial intelligence" itself, tracing its roots to the seminal Dartmouth Conference of 1956. This gathering of visionaries marked the inception of a field dedicated to creating machines capable of intelligent behavior. As we traverse through the subsequent decades, we witness the ebb and flow of enthusiasm, from the initial optimism to the "AI winter" and resurgence.

The chapter casts a spotlight on the pioneers who laid the foundation for AI's evolution. From Alan Turing's groundbreaking work to John McCarthy's coining of the term "artificial intelligence," we pay homage to the intellects whose ideas catalyzed the birth of a new era.

Advancements in symbolic AI, expert systems, and early machine learning take center stage, showcasing the diverse approaches taken in the pursuit of artificial intelligence. We explore landmark moments such as the development of the first chess-playing computer and the advent of expert systems like MYCIN, which heralded the potential for AI applications in specialized domains.

The narrative then unfolds into the era of neural networks, examining the resurgence of interest in machine learning and the foundational work of pioneers like Geoffrey Hinton. From the dawn of deep learning to the transformative impact of convolutional neural networks, we witnessed a paradigm shift that revitalized AI research.

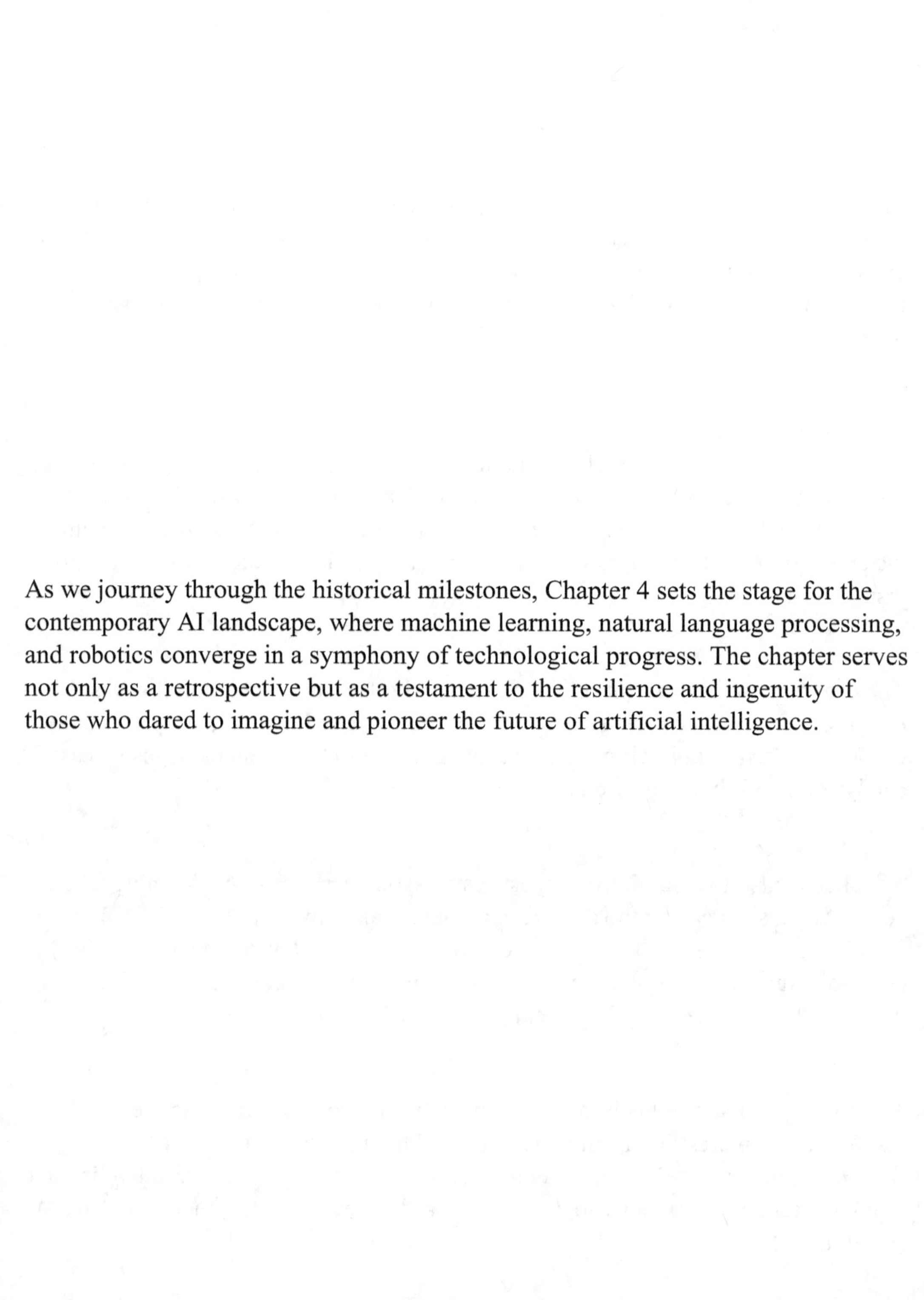

As we journey through the historical milestones, Chapter 4 sets the stage for the contemporary AI landscape, where machine learning, natural language processing, and robotics converge in a symphony of technological progress. The chapter serves not only as a retrospective but as a testament to the resilience and ingenuity of those who dared to imagine and pioneer the future of artificial intelligence.

CHAPTER FIVE

Navigating the Ethical Labyrinth: AI's Impact on Society

As artificial intelligence surges forward, Chapter 5 unravels the ethical considerations woven into the fabric of its advancements. In this exploration of the moral landscape, we confront the profound implications of AI on society, delving into questions that extend beyond algorithms and into the very essence of human values.

The chapter begins by probing the ethical dimensions of AI in decision-making processes. From automated systems influencing job opportunities to shaping criminal sentencing, we scrutinize the impact of algorithms on fairness, bias, and the delicate balance between efficiency and equity.

A deep dive into privacy concerns follows, examining the intersection of AI and surveillance technologies. As machine learning algorithms analyze vast datasets, the boundaries between public safety and personal privacy blur. We navigate the intricate web of facial recognition, data collection, and the potential for ubiquitous surveillance, raising critical questions about individual autonomy and the right to privacy.

The narrative then extends to the ethical responsibility of creators and developers. As AI systems become increasingly autonomous, who bears accountability for their actions? The chapter explores the ethical imperative of ensuring transparency, accountability, and the prevention of unintended consequences in the development and deployment of AI technologies.

Machine ethics takes center stage, challenging us to imbue artificial intelligence with ethical frameworks that mirror our societal values. Can we instill machines with a sense of morality, empathy, and an understanding of human ethical principles? The chapter grapples with the complexities of imbuing AI with a moral compass.

We conclude by scrutinizing the broader societal impacts of AI, from its influence on employment to its potential to exacerbate social inequalities. The ethical considerations surrounding AI's role in shaping the future of work and the distribution of resources prompt us to confront the responsibilities we bear as architects of this technological landscape.

Chapter 5 serves as a compass through the ethical labyrinth, urging us to consider not only the capabilities of AI but also the profound ethical choices that shape the society it co-creates.

CHAPTER SIX

Human-Centric Intelligence: Nurturing Strengths, Acknowledging Weaknesses

In the intricate dance between humans and machines, Chapter 6 unfolds the exploration of human-centric intelligence—the unique blend of strengths and vulnerabilities that define our cognitive landscape. This chapter delves into the innate qualities of human intelligence, juxtaposing them with the capabilities and limitations of artificial counterparts.

We commence by unraveling the tapestry of human cognition, celebrating the depth of emotional intelligence, creativity, and intuition. From the intricacies of social interaction to the nuanced understanding of cultural contexts, we delve into the qualities that distinguish human intelligence in a world teeming with technological marvels.

The chapter then turns its gaze toward the strengths that humans bring to the collaborative table. The ability to navigate ambiguity, make ethical decisions, and exhibit adaptability in complex, dynamic environments sets human intelligence apart. We explore the synergy that emerges when human intuition intertwines with the analytical power of AI, creating a potent combination that transcends the sum of its parts.

However, no exploration is complete without acknowledging the vulnerabilities woven into the fabric of human cognition. The chapter candidly explores the limitations of memory, susceptibility to cognitive biases, and the emotional dimensions that can introduce complexity into decision-making processes.

The narrative extends to the symbiotic relationships forming between humans and AI, where machines compensate for human limitations and vice versa. We scrutinize the delicate balance required to harness the strengths of both realms while mitigating the risks associated with over-reliance on one or the other.

As we navigate the landscapes of human-centric intelligence, the chapter prompts reflection on the profound responsibility borne by society in shaping the trajectory of AI. How can we leverage the strengths of human cognition to guide the development of AI systems that enhance rather than diminish the human experience? This exploration serves as a foundation for the chapters to come, where the interplay of strengths and weaknesses shapes the evolving narrative of intelligence in our rapidly changing world.

CHAPTER SEVEN

The Transformative Wave: AI's Impact on Employment

In the relentless surge of technological progress, Chapter 7 probes the seismic shifts underway as artificial intelligence reshapes the landscape of employment and the very fabric of the workforce. From automation to augmentation, this chapter unfolds the complex narrative of AI's influence on jobs, industries, and the evolving nature of work.

We commence with an exploration of the automation revolution, where machines equipped with AI capabilities undertake tasks traditionally performed by humans. From manufacturing to service sectors, we scrutinize the profound implications of efficiency gains and job displacement. The chapter navigates through historical precedents, drawing parallels between the current wave of automation and past industrial revolutions.

The narrative then pivots to the concept of augmentation—how AI empowers human workers by enhancing their capabilities. We explore scenarios where AI becomes a collaborative tool, enabling humans to focus on tasks that leverage their unique cognitive strengths while machines handle repetitive or data-intensive aspects of work.

A critical lens is applied to the impact on various sectors, examining how AI technologies redefine job roles, create new opportunities, and render some occupations obsolete. The chapter delves into the ethical dimensions of workforce transformation, addressing issues of equity, access to opportunities, and the responsibility of society to navigate this transition inclusively.

The exploration extends to the skills landscape, highlighting the imperative for upskilling and reskilling in the face of technological disruption. We examine the roles of education, industry, and policymakers in fostering a workforce that is adaptable, creative, and prepared for the challenges of the AI era.

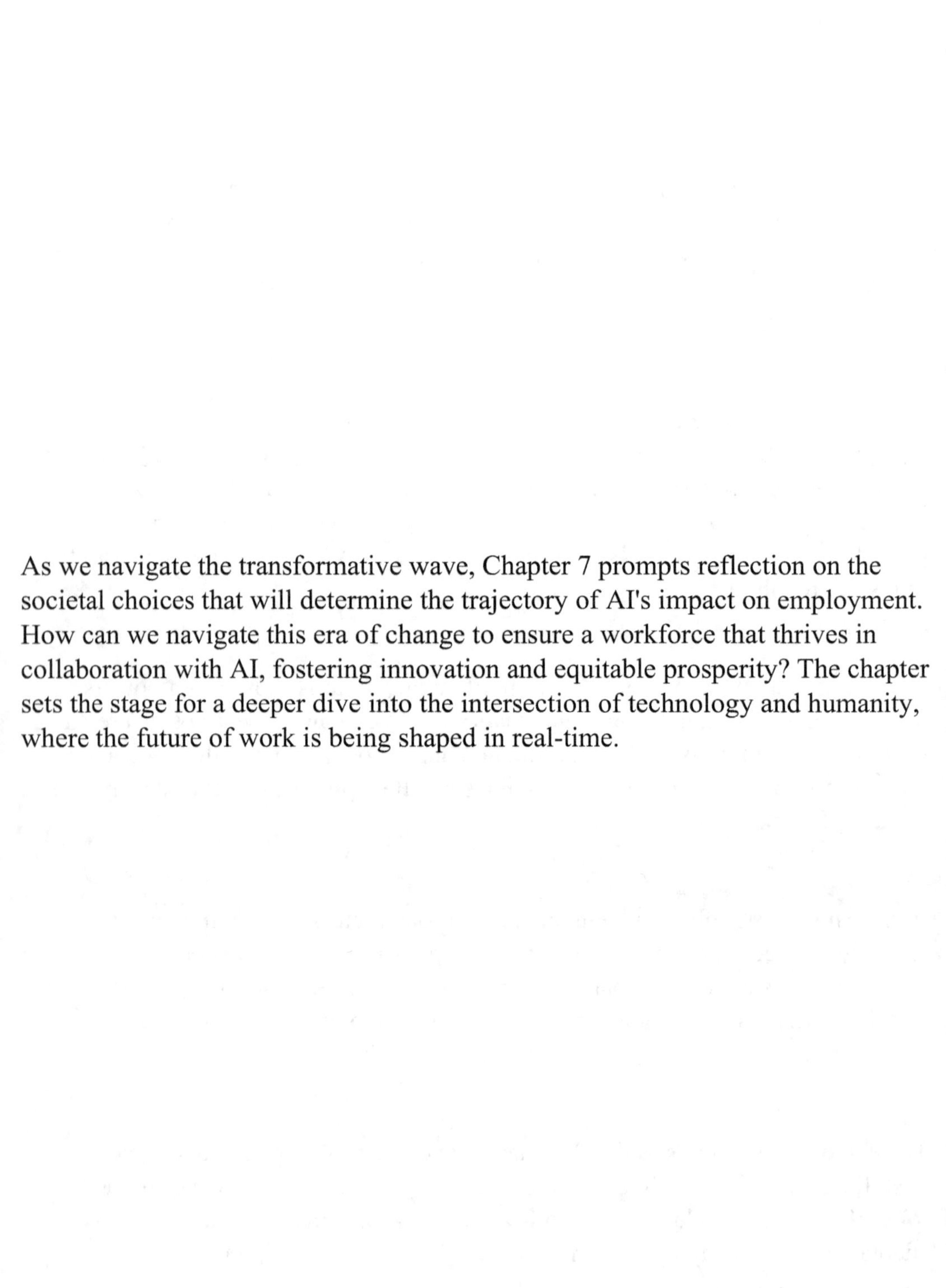

As we navigate the transformative wave, Chapter 7 prompts reflection on the societal choices that will determine the trajectory of AI's impact on employment. How can we navigate this era of change to ensure a workforce that thrives in collaboration with AI, fostering innovation and equitable prosperity? The chapter sets the stage for a deeper dive into the intersection of technology and humanity, where the future of work is being shaped in real-time.

Cognitive Synergy: Orchestrating Harmony in Human-AI Collaboration

In the ever-evolving symphony of intelligence, Chapter 8 unfurls the concept of cognitive synergy—a harmonious collaboration between humans and artificial intelligence that transcends individual capabilities. This chapter explores the transformative potential when human intuition and creativity intertwine with the analytical prowess of AI, creating a symphony of cognitive capabilities.

The journey begins by delving into real-world applications of human-AI collaboration, from healthcare diagnostics to creative endeavors. We scrutinize instances where the strengths of human cognition synergize with the computational power of AI, leading to breakthroughs that surpass what either could achieve in isolation.

The narrative navigates through the realms of decision-making, emphasizing the symbiotic relationships emerging as AI augments human judgment. Whether in business strategy or complex problem-solving, we explore scenarios where the amalgamation of human intuition and machine-driven insights leads to more informed, nuanced, and strategic decisions.

The chapter unfolds the concept of human-in-the-loop systems, where humans play a pivotal role in refining, validating, and guiding AI processes. From data annotation to algorithmic fairness, we examine how human oversight becomes a cornerstone in ensuring responsible and ethical AI applications.

As we explore cognitive synergy, the chapter addresses the challenges inherent in human-AI collaborations. Issues of transparency, trust, and understanding emerge as crucial elements in fostering effective partnerships. We examine how explainability in AI systems becomes pivotal, enabling humans to comprehend and trust the decisions made in collaboration with machines.

The narrative extends to the societal impacts of cognitive synergy, probing questions of accessibility, inclusivity, and the potential to bridge gaps in expertise. How can human-AI collaboration be harnessed to address complex global challenges, from healthcare disparities to environmental sustainability?

Chapter 8 serves as a canvas for envisioning a future where human-AI collaborations transcend the boundaries of what is currently conceivable. It prompts us to explore the vast landscape of possibilities when human and artificial intelligence join forces, fostering a synergy that propels us toward a future where the sum is truly greater than its parts.

CHAPTER NINE

Decoding Complexity: Machine Learning's Quest for True Understanding

In the intricate dance between data and algorithms, Chapter 9 embarks on a journey through the realms of machine learning—a powerful paradigm that seeks to unravel the complexities of our world. As we navigate the landscape of algorithms and data-driven insights, this chapter explores the quest for true understanding and the challenges encountered on this ambitious intellectual voyage.

The exploration commences by delving into the foundations of machine learning, from classical techniques to contemporary deep learning architectures. We scrutinize how algorithms, inspired by the human brain's neural networks, process vast amounts of data to discern patterns, make predictions, and ultimately, acquire a form of understanding.

The narrative unfolds into the nuances of supervised and unsupervised learning, showcasing the diverse approaches employed in the quest for true understanding. From image recognition to natural language processing, we examine real-world applications that demonstrate the transformative potential of machine learning across various domains.

As we traverse the landscape of algorithms, the chapter addresses the interpretability challenge—the inherent difficulty in comprehending the decision-making processes of complex machine learning models. We explore the imperative for explainable AI, where the black-box nature of algorithms becomes a critical consideration for both trust and accountability.

The quest for true understanding extends to the ethical dimensions of machine learning, probing issues of bias, fairness, and the responsible deployment of AI technologies. How do we navigate the ethical landscape as machines learn from human-generated data, inheriting both societal virtues and biases?

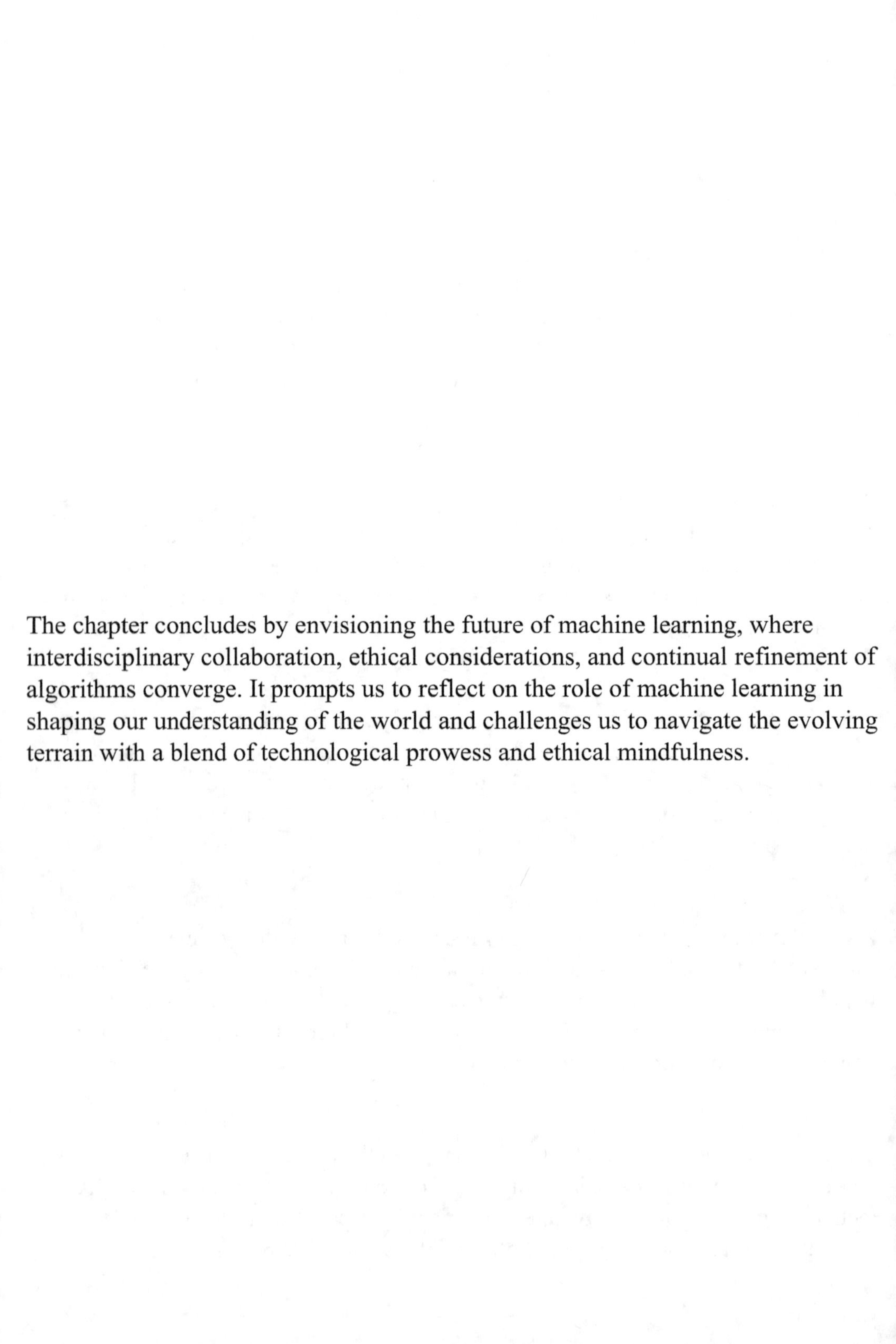

The chapter concludes by envisioning the future of machine learning, where interdisciplinary collaboration, ethical considerations, and continual refinement of algorithms converge. It prompts us to reflect on the role of machine learning in shaping our understanding of the world and challenges us to navigate the evolving terrain with a blend of technological prowess and ethical mindfulness.

CHAPTER TEN

Navigating Complexity: The Turing Dilemma Unveiled

As we stand at the crossroads of artificial and human intelligence, Chapter 10 unveils the intricacies of the Turing Dilemma—a conundrum that beckons us to explore the evolving relationship between machines and humanity. This chapter delves into the multifaceted dimensions of the dilemma, probing the challenges, opportunities, and ethical considerations that define the landscape of coexistence.

The journey begins by revisiting the essence of the Turing Test, reflecting on its historical significance and its role in shaping the discourse on artificial intelligence. We scrutinize the evolving criteria for intelligence, from early conversations with simple chatbots to the sophisticated language models that now seek to emulate human cognition.

The narrative extends to the broader implications of the Turing Dilemma, raising questions about the very nature of consciousness, self-awareness, and the ethical responsibilities entwined with creating intelligent machines. How do we define intelligence, and what criteria should guide our assessment of whether a machine truly possesses it?

The chapter explores the ethical considerations embedded in the Turing Dilemma, dissecting issues of agency, accountability, and the potential impact on societal structures. As machines approach human-like cognitive abilities, we confront the ethical imperative of ensuring that their deployment aligns with human values and societal well-being.

The narrative unfolds into scenarios where the Turing Dilemma intersects with real-world applications, from conversational agents to decision-making algorithms. We navigate the challenges posed by machines that simulate intelligence without genuine understanding, prompting us to question the ethical ramifications of creating entities that mimic cognitive capabilities.

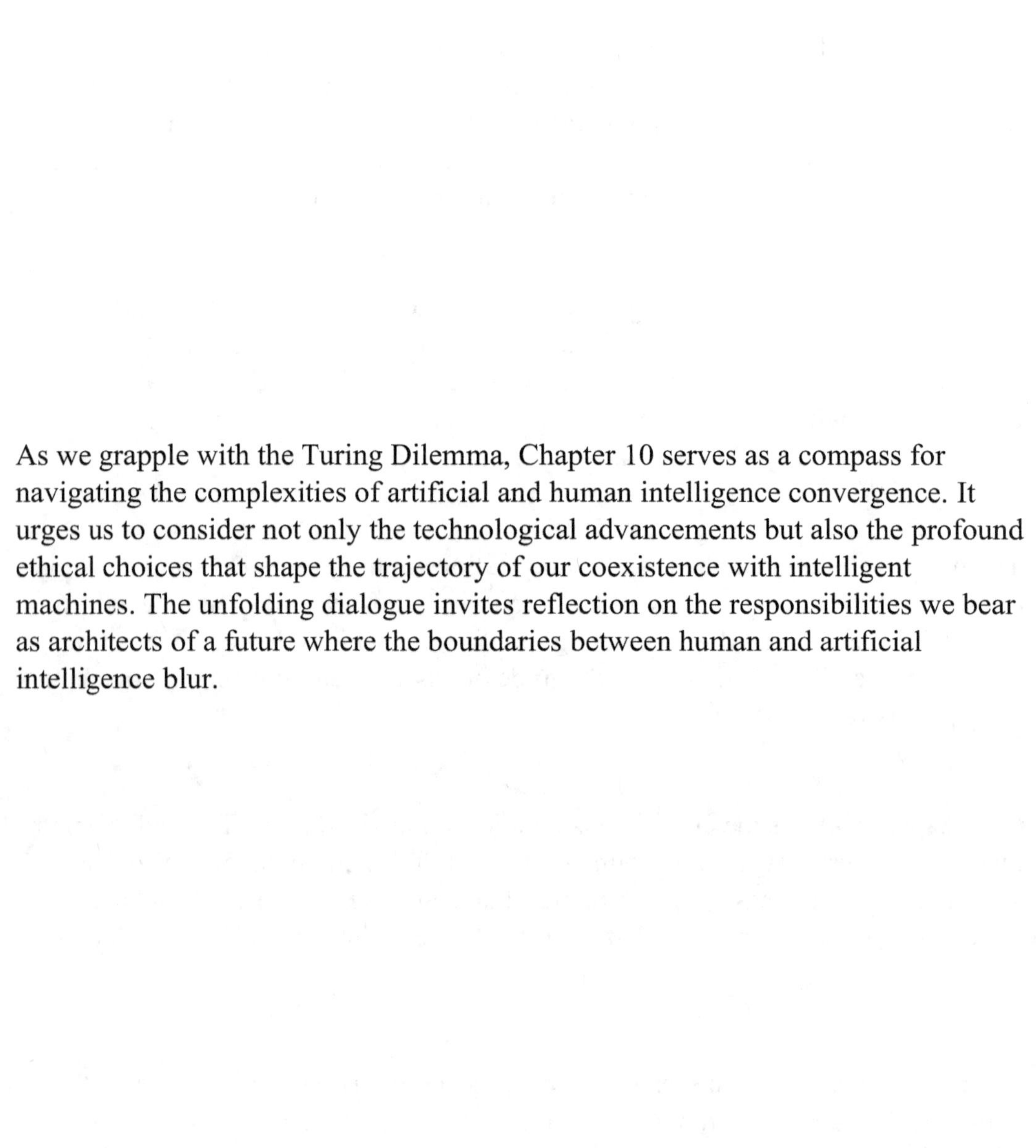

As we grapple with the Turing Dilemma, Chapter 10 serves as a compass for navigating the complexities of artificial and human intelligence convergence. It urges us to consider not only the technological advancements but also the profound ethical choices that shape the trajectory of our coexistence with intelligent machines. The unfolding dialogue invites reflection on the responsibilities we bear as architects of a future where the boundaries between human and artificial intelligence blur.

CHAPTER ELEVEN

The Ethical Crossroads: Navigating AI's Uncharted Societal Impact

As we venture further into the uncharted territories of artificial intelligence, Chapter 11 unravels the societal impact that accompanies the potential and risks inherent in AI's evolution. This chapter delves into the ethical crossroads where technological innovation meets the intricate fabric of human societies, prompting us to navigate the delicate balance between progress and responsibility.

The exploration begins with an examination of how AI is reshaping the social landscape. From the dynamics of communication to the fabric of social interactions, we scrutinize the transformative influence of intelligent algorithms on the way information is disseminated, opinions are formed, and communities are shaped.

As AI systems permeate various aspects of our lives, the chapter navigates the potential risks of reinforcing existing inequalities and biases. We delve into the ethical considerations of algorithmic decision-making, exploring how systemic biases in training data can perpetuate discrimination and inequity.

The narrative extends to the ethical responsibilities of organizations and policymakers in shaping the societal impact of AI. We scrutinize the need for transparent and inclusive decision-making processes, where the benefits and risks of AI technologies are weighed collectively, and the voices of diverse stakeholders are heard.

The chapter then explores the ethical considerations surrounding the use of AI in critical domains such as healthcare, education, and criminal justice. How do we ensure that AI technologies enhance access, equity, and fairness, rather than exacerbating existing disparities?

In navigating these ethical crossroads, the chapter prompts reflection on the role of individuals in the digital age. It challenges us to be informed and engaged participants in the ongoing dialogue about the societal impact of AI, advocating for ethical considerations that prioritize human values, dignity, and rights.

As we stand at the intersection of AI's potential and risks, Chapter 11 serves as a compass, guiding us through the complex terrain of uncharted societal impact. It encourages us to navigate with ethical foresight, ensuring that the promises of technological advancement align with the collective well-being of humanity.

<h1 style="text-align:center">CHAPTER TWELVE</h1>

Rethinking Societal Norms: Paradigms in the Era of Advanced Intelligence

In the transformative era of advanced intelligence, Chapter 12 delves into the shifting societal paradigms, exploring the profound impact that artificial intelligence has on the way we perceive, interact, and organize ourselves as a global community. This chapter navigates through the evolving landscapes of ethics, governance, and cultural norms in the wake of unprecedented technological advancements.

The exploration commences with a scrutiny of ethical considerations, probing the challenges and opportunities presented by AI. How do our moral frameworks adapt to accommodate the complexities of autonomous systems, and what ethical paradigms emerge as we navigate the intricate terrain of machine decision-making?

As AI becomes a pervasive force in governance and policymaking, the chapter unfolds the dynamics of regulatory frameworks and societal norms. From questions of privacy and security to the ethical implications of algorithmic governance, we navigate through the uncharted waters of shaping laws and policies that govern the intelligent systems that influence our daily lives.

The narrative extends to the cultural impact of advanced intelligence, exploring how AI technologies shape and redefine cultural norms, artistic expressions, and even the narratives that define our collective identity. We examine the interplay between technology and culture, considering how AI both reflects and influences societal values.

In this era of interconnectedness, the chapter scrutinizes the global impact of advanced intelligence on geopolitical dynamics and international relations. How does the proliferation of AI influence global collaboration, competition, and the distribution of power among nations?

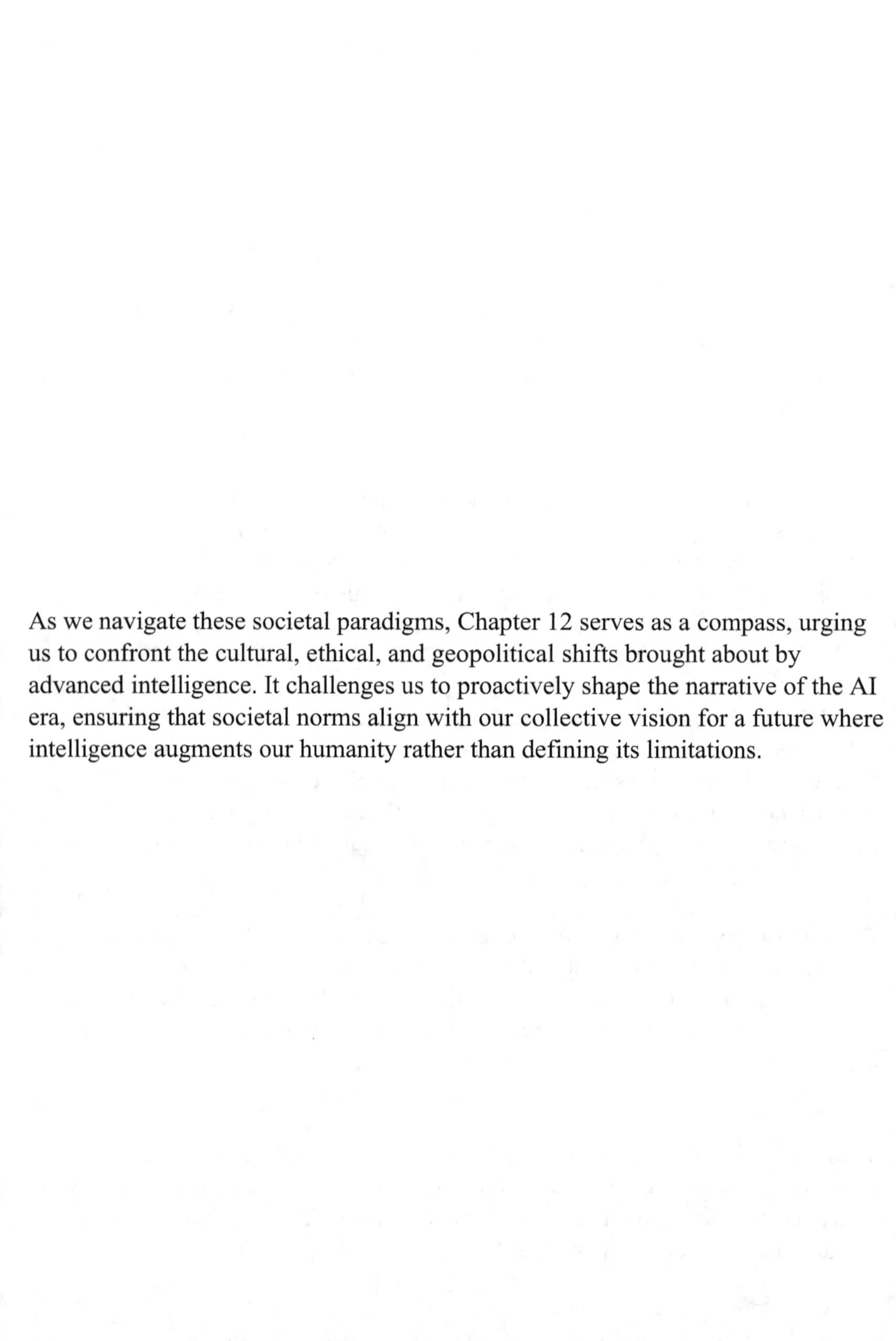

As we navigate these societal paradigms, Chapter 12 serves as a compass, urging us to confront the cultural, ethical, and geopolitical shifts brought about by advanced intelligence. It challenges us to proactively shape the narrative of the AI era, ensuring that societal norms align with our collective vision for a future where intelligence augments our humanity rather than defining its limitations.

CHAPTER THIRTEEN

Forging Pathways to Harmony: Strategies for Coexisting with Advanced Intelligence

As we stand at the threshold of the future, Chapter 13 delves into strategies for cultivating a harmonious coexistence between humanity and advanced intelligence. This concluding chapter explores pathways that lead us toward a future where the integration of artificial and human intelligence fosters not only technological innovation but also a flourishing society.

The exploration begins with an emphasis on interdisciplinary collaboration. As we navigate the complexities of advanced intelligence, we examine how fostering collaboration between technologists, ethicists, policymakers, and representatives from diverse fields can contribute to a holistic approach. Interdisciplinary dialogue becomes a cornerstone for addressing the multifaceted challenges and opportunities that lie ahead.

The narrative extends to the importance of education and literacy in the digital age. Strategies for enhancing public understanding of AI, its implications, and its potential empower individuals to make informed decisions. By cultivating a society that is well-versed in the language of technology, we lay the groundwork for responsible coexistence.

The chapter advocates for proactive governance and ethical frameworks. Strategies for crafting policies that ensure transparency, fairness, and accountability in AI applications become imperative. By involving communities in the decision-making.

Charting a Course Beyond the Turing Dilemma

In the closing chapters of "The Turing Dilemma: Navigating the Future of Artificial and Human Intelligence," we've embarked on a journey through the intricate interplay between human and artificial intelligence. The Turing Dilemma, a central theme woven throughout our exploration, has prompted us to confront questions of intelligence, consciousness, and the ethical responsibilities that accompany the rise of machines.

As we reflect on the chapters that unfolded, from understanding intelligence and assessing machine capabilities to exploring historical milestones and ethical implications, we find ourselves at a pivotal juncture. The Turing Dilemma, with its roots in Alan Turing's visionary test, has served as a guiding light through the uncharted territories of AI's evolution.

The exploration of human-centric intelligence, cognitive synergy, and the societal paradigms shaped by AI has illuminated the potential for collaboration between humans and machines. We've witnessed the transformative power of machine learning, navigated the impact on employment, and contemplated the ethical considerations embedded in the very fabric of AI development.

In the face of uncharted territories, we've grappled with the potential and risks, acknowledging the profound influence AI holds over societal norms and global dynamics. As we conclude this journey, the question that lingers is not whether AI will replace human intelligence but how we will navigate this coexistence, ensuring it is ethical, inclusive, and beneficial for all.

Charting a course beyond The Turing Dilemma requires collective efforts. Interdisciplinary collaboration, educational initiatives, and proactive governance emerge as strategies to shape a future where advanced intelligence augments our humanity rather than diminishes it. The responsibility lies not only with technologists and policymakers but with each individual who contributes to the societal dialogue on AI.

As we stand on the precipice of this AI-infused future, the Turing Dilemma serves not as an obstacle but as a catalyst for thoughtful consideration. The journey ahead invites us to leverage the potential of AI while safeguarding against risks, foster cognitive synergy that enhances human capabilities, and navigate societal changes with ethical foresight.

In this concluding chapter, we envision a future where the Turing Dilemma becomes a beacon guiding us toward a harmonious coexistence—a future where the integration of artificial and human intelligence enriches the tapestry of our collective experience. The choices we make today will shape the contours of this future, and as we close this chapter, the challenge and opportunity before us lie in navigating this future with wisdom, empathy, and a commitment to the well-being of humanity.